Zac and the

Story by Jackie Tidey
Photography by Lindsay Edwards

Rigby®
A Harcourt Achieve Imprint

www.Rigby.com
1-800-531-5015

Here come Zac and Dad.

Here come the ducks.

"Dad," said Zac.

"Look at the ducks.

The ducks are hungry."

"The ducks are looking for bread," said Zac.

Dad said to Zac,

"Look in my bag."

Zac looked in the bag.

"Here is bread
for the ducks," said Zac.

"Here you are, hungry ducks,"

said Zac.

Zac said to the ducks,

"I am hungry, too."

Dad looked in the bag.

"Here you are, hungry Zac,"

said Dad.